the room within

Other poetry books by Moore Moran

Iron Leaves (chapbook)

Firebreaks (winner of the National Poetry Book Award for 1999)

the room within

poems | moore moran

swallow press | athens, ohio

Swallow Press / Ohio University Press, Athens, Ohio 45701
www.ohioswallow.com

To obtain permission to quote, reprint, or otherwise reproduce or
distribute material from Swallow Press / Ohio University Press publications,
please contact our rights and permissions department at (740) 593-1154 or
(740) 593-4536 (fax).

Printed in the United States of America
Swallow Press / Ohio University Press books are printed on acid-free paper ⊗ ™

18 17 16 15 14 13 12 11 10   5 4 3 2 1

Acknowledgments
The author thanks the editors of the following magazines
where some of these poems were first published:

America ("Outside Truckee" and "When You Return"); *Atlantic Monthly* ("Rimbaud: On His Muse" and "That Breakfast"); *Beloit Poetry Journal* ("Les Derniers Jours d'Eloise"); *Candelabrum* ("On Wyeth's *Below Dover*"); *Chicago Review* ("6:30 Mass"); *First Things* ("Holy Thursday" [original title, "Tonight I Asked You In"], "Ordinary Time in the Pews," and "To the Golden Gate Bridge"); *New Compass* ("When Paris Lay at Helen's Side"); *New Criterion* ("Late in the Night"); *New Letters* ("Dog Days in Puerto Vallarta"); *Paris Review* ("Horseman, 5:14"); *Poetry Monthly* (UK) ("Above Santa Cruz"); *Raintown Review* ("Silent Night" and "The Room Within"); *Sequoia* ("Sleeping Beauty," "Those Who Pray for Us," "*Sunday Movie,*" and "Somebody's Mother's Good Blanket" [original title, "A Hair Too Loud"]); *Texas Review* ("Monterey County" I–VIII); *Threepenny Review* ("Four" and "Ord"); *Yale Review* ("The Face").

E-zines: For Poetry ("Just Joking" and "My Poem in the Lobby at Hewlett-Packard"); *New Formalist* ("Utah Dawn"); *Three Candles* ("Home Sick"); *Hyper Texts* for various earlier published poems.

Library of Congress Cataloging-in-Publication Data
Moran, Moore.
The room within : poems / Moore Moran.
    p. cm.
ISBN 978-0-8040-1128-0 (acid-free paper) — ISBN 978-0-8040-1129-7
(pbk. : acid-free paper) — ISBN 978-0-8040-4043-3 (electronic)
I. Title.
PS3563.O7663R66 2010
811'.54—dc22

2010000614

To Pat, and to the memory

of our daughter, Noel, 1960–2009

. . . Far up in the stretches of night; night splits and
the dawn breaks loose;
I, through the terrible novelty of light, stalk on,
stalk on . . .

—*Yeats*

contents

part one

part two

part one

Winter Arriving

Down garden wall
at dusk today
a sparrow, bending
in a wild fall,
at my boot lay,
making his ending.

Onto my thumb
his blood welled brown
staining my gaze;
I lingered numb
in the ice and haze
through which he'd flown

his final burst.
Roused by dark's hush
I laid him away,
then heard the first
calls from the brush
where sparrows stay.

To the Golden Gate Bridge

In 1942 when I was ten
and you were five, we got together Sundays
as I'd head north to military school,
flagging the Greyhound down. Those were not fun days:

Mother, broken by life, had left the scene;
Pearl had called father to a four-year fight.
My scruffy boots, the tell-all uniform,
spotted and rank-less, put on view the fright

I was at fifth-grade soldiering. Then I heard
through open windows how you'd worked it out—
towers in the wind, singing above the sea,
anthems of self-belief, innate, devout—

and you became a brother instantly.
As weeks passed and I listened on that span,
your riffs of joy seemed almost tuned to ease
a child's fear of growing into a man.

Some, you did not convince as easily.
May they, drenched in despair, who could not heal,
return to light somewhere down harbor skies,
beyond the flotsam and the listening seal.

Bees

The hive whines in the oak above the pool,
A rotted enclave yet a natural home
For these small gatherers. First light, they fly,
Some favoring alyssum, others mums,
A few charmed by an open Pepsi can
Left near a lawn chair by my tanning daughter.

Toward noon, in quiet shallows, I see them
Slowing, circling, freighted with heat and hoard;
Some, visibly spent, totter to water's edge
And tumble in, wings crying urgent signals—
Two, three, at a time I fish them from
Bright pulsing circles of would-be demise.

They do me no harm, for by now they know
The clumsy hulk attending them is friendly;
They wait to be redeemed, set on the deck,
Dazed, upright and happy for another day.
And yet they drop in numbers far too great
To save them all. The dying, without further

Protest, wait numb and motionless to pass
Back into nature. Such is an aging fancy,
Guileless enough to solemnize these passings.
The bee man wants the hive; he plans at dusk
To call on the queen—get her take on moving
To solid, more considered royal turf.

The Face

As long ago as Atlantis
we remember your face
at the south window
of the palace, sending
banner-spanned
festival streets below
into fresh hysteria.

And later in Prague
how you swam for
the communists, toppling
record after world record,
then standing for the press,
a dripping goddess.

We have seen you
in the plum-dark desert
just before dawn, walking
with a gas can, your hair-
lights mirroring the new sky
like eyes of immigrants.

Mostly these moments escaped
into dim frescos, or
grainy photographs
or easy sentimental poems,

leaving us to imagine
how the Hunter must have felt
losing you that day
in the Greek forest,
his astonished fingers
shrinking from your laurel neck.

Late in the Night

Late in the night I dreamed I was to die,
to see through change to the unchanging season
where love is said to live and reign (blue sky
is for the called no less than for the chosen).
My love lay with me softly, murmuring
in sleep of cherished seasons come and gone,
sweet passings which in time soured, corrupting
our hands and lips and eyes. Who to atone?
Between two worlds I hovered, tried to hedge,
but no scheme came, only the terror in
surrendering what I am, heartbreak serrating
awareness to a raw and mortal edge,
and I, dense tangle of transgressions, waiting
for the dark, the accusation or the grin.

My Poem in the Lobby at Hewlett-Packard

A Steuben ashtray blinked disdainfully,
Daring my Kool to near; my lyric hope
Lay buried there on coffee table oak.
I knew the *Atlantic* by an exposed corner
Of quiet masthead poised beneath the shout
Of well-thumbed *Newsweek,* much-respected *Forbes.*
No need of exhumations, I had seen
The comers' page where Plath's poem paired with mine:
Heraldings of exiles yet to come.

Truth was our hope of haven then, not death
Nor the false calm of corporate mooring posts,
Yet there I sat in a sea of Tyrian shag,
My interview splashing out to anchor me.
In recommended pitch I bobbed and belled:
Impassive fraudulent energy for hire.

Near the Veterans' Mental Hospital

They straggle out for their sundown stroll,
all heading in different directions
like strangers leaving a horror film.

A kid with lines on his face
huddles inside himself, eyes spinning
like a transported Jolson;
any moment you expect him to theatrically go
to one knee, do Mammy.

Curbside, staffed and bearded Little John
cordially directs forest traffic
into an ice cream parlor. Unheeded,
he finger-scolds the merry band
of Hondas prancing by.

A bird-legged black in robe and slippers
confronts a defunct mailbox, banging
for access, whistling as if his trembling hand
were young and dry. His letter
has no stamp, envelope blank as his gaze.

O, mischief of madness! A blurred
disquietude to those commuting through—
to neighbors standing hostage in their windows,
the non-negotiable sovereignty of nonsense.

Rimbaud and His Muse

Black birches full of autumn sound—
like rain their few excited leaves;
what honest passion can be found
where light dissembles, touch deceives?

Between the trees she comes and leaves
shaken to learn of my seclusion—
I cannot ease the loss she grieves,
I built my art upon illusion.

The calm she looks for in my figure
restraint or death itself conceives;
through my long dream I trusted neither:
blind will alone confronts the leaves.

My skill was stronger than the leaves
and yet it falls away as fast;
she frowns and waits and disbelieves
that madness found me out at last.

Beside her now my shadow heaves
like meaning seen but never formed,
hugely alert among the leaves
where worse than madness is performed.

Sunday Movie

Sunday and the ranch shut down under
A hell sun, breaking even the flies' schedule—
They circle the silent harvester,
Circle again. Scatter.

The men have gone to town to cool off, and Perk,
Foreman's wife, stands in the kitchen window
Working up rhubarb pie, her lips dusty red like
The pulp in her hands.

Over to the river where manzanita fights to
Catch its breath, I sit in the last of the moving
Water, letting cool fingers crawl up
The legs of my jeans.
Perk calls over there's an Abbott & Costello film
Revival going on in King City, a howl
According to the papers. Why don't I flag down the bus?
I look like I could use a laugh
(My lonesome showing again).

Dusty and doorless, an hour late as usual,
The bus floats up out of a two-lane
Mirage, windows gone, radio blaring "Linda Mujer,"
And twenty Mexicans in clean shirts and dresses
Politely study the floorboards as I climb through.
There's a seat near the back next to

A knockout Consuelo who's brought her sewing along
And nods that it's okay for me to sit next to her.
Her eyes are soft as a deer's, and I do my best
Not to notice she's adrift in cologne.

I go for pleasant, piecing it together in broken Spanish,
Telling her I'm a ranch rat headed for a Sunday movie,
And where's she bound for on such a pleasant day?
Slowly she raises those gentle eyes from her sewing
And in perfect English says that her father is seated
Directly behind me so don't try anything cute.

Hydroplane

Through phantom ferns
    intrudes the real.
We listen as it burns,
    wails, like an axe
honing on distant wheel.
    Night is lifting.

Presently, muted slaps
    of tide arouse
the dreaming shore. Teal gaps
    between arched leaves
flare with first shoots of sun,
    and a glitter heaves,

slashing across the glass
    grindstone. Sudden
metallic flanks flash past,
    sending a spire
of prism'd gems aloft,
    smacking like fire.

Four

To Boo

I can remember four
all because of two nights.
Mother and Father moved
into a Spanish house
that year. We came loosely
bundled after midnight,
down the alkaline road
south, so long, so fiery.
Big Eva, Dutch nanny,
read icy tales from Grimm
till the indigo sky
went black in the high car
window . . . motoring dreams.
Two pillow-minded drunks,
my sister and I reeled
through echoing cool rooms
to fall in shadowy beds.

It was a run-hide house
with a pomegranate tree
in the old court below
where the wind never came.
Within a week, the red
below my room (that no-
red-like-it red) took me,

with its tart seeds, fast friends
so that afterward when

the circus stopped outside
and I could not come down,
having been bad that day,
but high over the court
watched them in their costumes,
after supper singing
out through the tall rose gate,
up the around-town hill,
the pomegranate tree was
bleeding in the dusk,
redder than the clown's mouth
and redder than Rose Red.

View from a Barcelona Hotel Room

The park sits in shadows, empty.
Siesta heat, the stillness of the trees
Reclaim the square.

A child's swing arcs to and fro.
No child anywhere.

For a moment the swing will recall
Somebody small.

Home Sick

Called in sick today, the Irish soul
in me clamoring for intensive care.
Slouched in November Park, I watch
cold needles of sun prick
bench and pathway; scribbles
of wind tighten the sparrow's wing,
the bellies of camellias.
Where Sunday's children took
seesaw laughter from the knoll,
Dandelions spring, shiver.

Why is it we, eternally twin-pregnant
it seems, with fear, self-doubt,
look to parks for a soul douche
when parks, miracles of aloofness,
ever prefer appearances: the huff
of puffball poodle, the arrogant
amble of the gaunt-hearted?

Across in porch shadows, a solitary
teenage black rocks her fitful
child. I sense her acceptance,
and, like her quieting babe,
feed on the genius of her calm.
Faintly she smiles at me,
a frieze for late autumn: three
exiled by a town at work, rather
more together than not,
as home sick souls incline.

Low Tide at Loreto

Where we go face-down in masks
Coral hums up sea surprises,
Stained-glass slivers, instinct-triggered,
Shying round us, questioning—
A light-year foot away.
Rainbow platys hang in ranks:
Like medals on Mexican generals.

Climbing late from sauna seas
We walk the widening half-mile back
Past reef now bare and dripping,
Pubic thicket on shore's pale belly.
Texturing nightfall: the brush of your hip
Subtle as the tide's turning.

The Room Within

Cold builds against the room within,
burns in the walls and in the bone:
a glacial shadow stealing in.
He crafts a plea to the unknown.

The still hours pall, surrender's work.
Attentively, through alien blear,
uncertainty and terror lurk.
He senses no deliverance here

where numbered days begin their slowing,
and faces toward the bedside loom.
He's part of here and part of going,
an empty room within a room.

Sir Walter Raleigh to His Wife

Based on a letter written the dawn of his expected execution, 1603

Dear Besse, receive the last words I shall speak.
My love I send upon a life of thanks
For your privations taken for my sake;
Though now, dear, look to help your strange descent,
The rights of your poor child through my dispraise.
And for the love you bore me while I lived,
Do not now hide yourself for many days:
Your tears cannot avail me, I am dust.

When I am gone, no doubt you will be sought
By many, for the world thinks I was rich;
Ignore the pretense (even that must be bought):
O anguish ever is the end when one
Becomes a prey and afterwards despised.
The sight of my blade-shattered throat should free
The hateful, cowardly choler which, disguised,
Would kill you with an extreme poverty.

To what friend you can turn I do not know,
For all of mine have left me where I wait;
How sad it is to be surprised with death—
I cannot leave you in a sure estate.
But can you live secure, care for no more,
The rest is vanity. Besse, love God well
And soon begin to repose yourself on Him:
The constant love immense and personal.

For when you have prolonged your dignity
Under the closing dark of hurt and loss,

You shall sit down by sorrow in the end.

And teach our son to love and dread the cross,
That he grow up in Him who gains us all;
Then will His love restore what hate withdrew—
A husband and a father to your son,
A presence this world cannot take from you.

Though for your fierce concern I begged my life,
I must condemn myself in such escapes;
Know that your Raleigh dies a resolute man,
Despising death and all its ugly shapes.
I can't write more. I hardly steal this time
While others sleep. He is beyond all harms
Who chose and loved you in his happiest days.
Now let my just God hold you in His arms.

That Breakfast

In memory of Wallace Stevens

His pigeons have reached darkness
By now, and absolute shade,
The one fast color, hardened
The rich change of his blue gaze.

Indelible leaves falling
Across the Sundays, firing
An ice-rimmed sky or blazing
In his page, will hold his sound.

Earth only will find him cold.

How fair must have been that late
And inexorable stand
When, closely groomed, breakfasting
Expensively on warm wine,
Eggs Benedict, he reworked
Some dark juxtaposition,

His gaze led by innocence,
His hands in the moment, all
Malice suspended softly,
And heard in the seventh hour,
Dilating like the sea's prose,
That long formality: peace.

On Wyeth's *Below Dover*

A nameless sloop in sedge grass points
Off toward a sea the sand dune hides,
The blue leached from her hull and joints,
Her cabin echoing old tides

That curled her here to tamer winds.
Her boom protests but little: short
Jibes shudder to corrosive ends.
Forgotten in the local port,

She leans like deafness to the cry
Of summering children come to race
Her decks with games of "Capt'n Bligh,"
Till dusk-borne dinner bells sound truce.

The silence holds. A humid moon
Visits her hull then climbs away
To light, atop a nearby dune,
Her sightless march into decay.

Boo at Seventeen

How quietly she lives,
A little lonely, a little proud,
Like a foreign girl on exchange.

Do not confuse her silence with disdain
Or her high carriage with indifferent powers—
Warnings merely of wary family genes.

Her ears are open for the sounds of love.
Favors lurk in her eyes.

Walking

Sometimes when I am walking,
I become afraid of walking
Out on myself.

Oh, I know, surely,
I walk myself with me
Wherever I go, still I marvel
At how much of me
Remains behind.

M^{use}

Cherry-hard young I was
   when first you bedded me
and did the things lust does.
   Though you lived fast and free

I was not one who sought
   new faces or new ends,
hungry for what you taught:
   the tyranny, the amends.

Of late, you're back again
   (no new lads to uncover?)
demanding I maintain
   some semblance of the lover;

Listen, I held your heat
   risking all to defend it!
Old now, I cannot cheat
   the silence that must end it.

So let it end in sleep,
   the spectral with the human;
what goddess cares to keep
   at love's expense love's union?

You'd think I might have learned,
   having done Hell and burned.

Custom House Cafe stood on this spot, straddling
Pier and seawall like a fisherman gaffing catch.
It was here, in '46 that Carlos brought pizza
To the county—hand-pounding his dough flats so fine
That when he spun them at the ceiling, light
From the harbor shone through.

At the great iron oven he would hand them out crackling,
Bubbling real Mafia mozzarella,
Tomato so fresh it sassed you all the way down;
Crust edges: buttery popover. Friday nights,
Ramirez and I downed two extra-larges per, hardly pausing
To pull on longnecks so cold chunks of ice

Still knocked around inside the bottles. Today
You can only get pizza at the franchise parlors in town
Where the freshest thing going is the waiters.
And nobody tosses anymore. Instead, they pancake
Their wheat-germy dough through rubber wringers
Lifted from old washing machines in the junkyard.

Those Who Pray for Us

Old windbreaker stuffed for warmth with pages
Torn from *Parade's End,* I bed down on the stormy
Point near the monastery
Where Carmelite nuns kneel behind stone walls
In their tiny cells, praying for us
As they will always.

No light in the wall shows,
Only the rain and the wind, but you can
Feel them in there praying in the dark.
One with a silver voice begins to sing
Low and soft and steady, and I fall asleep
Dreaming of the promises of God for his people.

Dawn arrives fresh from the mountains,
Staining the ocean sands with peaches, golds.
At cliff's edge I wave to two college girls out early
Chasing a weekend tan. They wave me down,
So I skid pebbled red rock.

They're nice kids, up from Hollister and horny,
Looking to get with boys.
When they see I'm bumming it they offer
Coffee from a thermos and ask about the town.

I tell them another hour and the footballs

And Frisbees will be sailing, and they'll
Have their pick of Stanford's virulent, so just

To wait and get their faces and laughter ready.
Sly smiles.

       What was I doing, they want to know,
Up on the point. I explain about the nuns
And they are amazed to learn that sort of thing
Still goes on in this day and age. Then they roll
On their tummies, open their bras, and wait
For the sun and scene to gain momentum.

The Gypsies

After Baudelaire

The tribe, prophetic, showing wine-raw eyes,
Left yesterday, the children piggyback
Or at the patient breast: hoard that complies
With playfulness or hunger or with slack.
Beside the carts, battered by time and miles,
The men on foot go, each with a brass gun,
Their wily faces quick with forebears' smiles,
Who, like them, lived by flimflam on the run.

The cricket listening on the barren lea
Sings louder as they pass, and Cybele
Who always loved them summons a new moss
To the charred rocks, and fashions a few flowers
Before their feet as once again they cross
The ancestral empire of unscheduled hours.

Ordinary Time in the Pews

Ordinary days again.
Advent, Pentecost are past;
who now will accept our sins,
raise the dust in which we're cast?

Cold the God flesh on the tree,
banned the crèche to attic murk,
sheer the silence after prayer,
Nothing seems at all to work.

Yet we try and try again
serving Him we hardly know:
honk if you love Jesus, friend,
beeping blessings as we go.

Here we meet who, somehow, must
rescue meaning from the dust,
where betrayal's kiss presents
our best hope of relevance.

Les Derniers Jours d'Eloise

Beside the wall in yellowed linen,
Where stone engenders fall and spring,
She cannot but mistake as human
The heartbeat of each living thing.

From pity in another place,
Abelard, come to mind alone,
Still wore his manhood in his face
Till mind and all went back to bone.

And beauty that she scarcely gave,
Now past contagion or demands,
Can find in stone the heart to save
A love it no more understands.

At last, bewildered dignity,
Filmed thin upon the aging bone
Relents, and all her losses flee
In shadows lengthening from stone.

Now days themselves are but the sound
Of love lines endlessly begun
In mind, unmoved and unprofound,
Smoothing against oblivion.

Somebody's Mother's Good Blanket

They park their fuchsia Bug
Next to my heap, making us
The only two cars in the lot,

And head out toward the surf
Where I lie reading. They flap down somebody's
Mother's good blanket and that makes
Us the only two parties on a gray beach.

Casually these high school couples
Look through me—a drift log chosen
To anchor them in the wind.

First things first. They crank up
The ghetto blaster, open four beers and, talking
Of the Stones and of the Dead,
Peel to the buff.

The blonde has boobs like cucumbers,
Ass flat as Sudan; the redhead,
All hips and stomach, resembles
A Bosc pear; standard beanpole
The boys, knees and teeth mostly.

The four perch, all talking at once,
Looking every place but at me and each
Other, their voices steadily rising like

A robe of sound to cover them in
Their push toward identity.
They do not touch each other, and their beers
Stand full and forgotten.

They are laughing a hair too loud,
And though I'm rooting for them,
Goose bumps are sprouting everywhere.
They're not pulling it off at all.

When Paris Lay at Helen's Side

When Paris lay at Helen's side,
and she was lightning on his limbs,
few doubted such authority
would finally tame him.

And he was hers in bed, in war,
in revelry, in argument;
her femaleness drenching his wits
with endless want.

So what becomes of long devotion
when suddenly death takes the lover?
A harvest lost? Is passion mortal?
Does promise weather?

It's said that every hundred years
Helen returns to tend his urn,
that in chill walls of Trojan bronze
the dust yet burns.

Utah Dawn

Like piled books the mesas lie,
their pages dark, convincing, spare,
unedited raw history
shrinking the soul that wanders here.

The sky throbs, quickens and unfolds
great limbs of light that shock the air
to living pulse. Cold shelf lands glare;
a stern library silence holds.

Alert and panting on the butte,
the wolf awakens to her thirst;
in hunt's expectancies immersed,
she quickly scents the alien boot,

and reads the bighorn and the hare,
archives astir, and tinged by hues
of river mist from canyon floor,
lurks deep in rainbows that can bruise.

Outside Truckee

I see him in his window, old man
With a blue face,
Standing deeper and deeper
Like a mountain pool at the end of a long rain.
He stirs only within himself.
A late reach of winter light
Coaxes from under a neighboring porch
Two dusty cats
He might surround with warmth
If he could catch.
Tentative migrants drift in
From country roads as the wood town
Lights up for the night.
Few voices reach him. Few sounds.
Only the canyon wind sanding the premises.
A soft tumult in his raccoon eyes,
He marks the passing of the year
Upon the land.

Star Dust

Occasions that occasion us
expend a self-consuming force
sometimes called love. The ancient fuss
survives the cramped seats of a Porsche,

spats in the bridal sheets, the chafe
of autumn hill-grass, anywhere
the flesh conspires to get off
in damp relief or dry despair.

Yearn is another term for breathing.
Hostage, we live on cruising wheels,
eye ever quick, need ever seething,
rejections linger . . . unrung bells.

We trust our immortality
To sex, its produce and its scars,
and so persists the roundelay,
this dance of dust among the stars.

When You Return

You were here moments ago pruning mums,
Bursts of vanilla on cool stems.

Across the lawn a Rain Bird fans, tapping soft welts
Along my page. The tea is pale with ice.

When you return, though your step make no sound,
I'll sense the richness without lifting my eyes.

part two

Monterey County I

Scent of cypress gusting cliffs,
Black gulls sit on the sea,
Sun a part of it and not.
Everywhere sea thunder.
A draught of autumn month on end.

Like every native boy,
I heartily climb these rocks
As fat as kings, and study
The momentary pools
Composed no more of water
Than wind, and for hours take
The rock crab's view of things.

M onterey County II

Foundering windmills creak
A few stiff turns at the sky,
Pumping only the rising fog
Of afternoon. Time and again
They are halting to check
Their joints for life.

The old barns, bleached
And battered by a century of fury
From the sea, still breathe
Through their scars. They groan
And sway like alcoholics,
Dazed at the unguessed
Emptiness of years.

Monterey County III

Wet moon dries in the dawn . . .
huge pelicans tuck into swords,
plunge, gorge on the anchovy wave.
All a-flap, sea-sister terns—
too slight to muscle a share—
crowd feast after feast,
lighting the offshore tides in tangle-flash.

Sated, the sword birds disengage,
work up a crystal morning sky
amid a thousand scolding cries.
The little terns tuck into daggers
stabbing the empty wave
in outraged imitation.

Monterey County IV

Into our sky
Thunderheads clatter
Like giant ice blocks
To a punch bowl.

With thunder, rain, wind.
Stingers of cold ream the black
Furrows of the fields
And blast the sagged barley;
Thatch-ruffled goats wait it out
On the hill.

We walk tumid earth,
You small, glistening,
Holding my thoughts
As if they were my hand.

Monterey County V

High on the cliff
I watch a black pelican
Crouched in the rocks
Below the wind.
Oil-soaked, mustard
Seed eye
Trained on my cliff,
He's making his stand.

As the wind drops,
He calls out, flopping
Toward flight, keeping
At it till the night
And the sea claim him—
One more loose rock
Awash.

Monterey County VI

I could tell you
Of a kitchen in Castroville
Where love once lived,
Then hardened like
A dishcloth in sill frost.

Monterey County VII

Strawberry pinks and clarets
Quilt the valley as far as eye can see,
To the first pined upturnings
Of the mountains of Santa Lucia.
Along the potholed two-lane,
Tailgates down for the harvest,
Old pickups doze under new paint:
Canary yellow, patent leather black.

Teeth flash in Latino heads
Bent to the picking;
They appear to see only the work
Of their hands. I know better,
Waving Godspeed as I trespass
Through the birthright of their silence.

Monterey County VIII

Tomorrow I'll head up
To Watsonville
And drink with a Mexican
Widow I know;

Later
In side streets,
The drinking and
Lying done with,

We'll listen to
The leather sounds
Of the old houses
Riding easily
By the artichoke fields
Under the wind;

When the wind quickens,
Blowing the moon down,
We'll scoot through
Our misgivings
To her fire.

Ord

In boot camp at Ord everybody was dead serious
About the training
As the war ground down to a
Terminal idle that still chewed up kids.
There were a thousand tricks to learn in those
Sixteen weeks, packed tighter than a Pound canto.

Gradually I saw that just two skills
Relative to the rank of private
Were going to get me through the moment
And whatever might come after:
Shooting straight and staying anonymous.

So I perfected myself in the care and firing
Of that edgy equalizer, the MI rifle,
And slept whenever I could through the rest of it.

And it turned out in the platoon I had a clone
—Same height, weight, eye color, and so forth—
Named Morgan. Put fatigues on us
And our mothers couldn't tell us apart,
So naturally the cadre
Was constantly mistaking us too.

I'd stay out of sight and he'd yell, "Morgan,
Clean the shit cans!" or "Morgan, police
The wrappers—let's see some ass and elbows!"

And Morgan, the poor bastard, plodded
Week after week through this plain
Case of mistaken identity and never did catch on.

The last day, when we were fully trained and terrified,
The cadre said, "Well, Morgan, how does it feel
To be a killing machine?"
I told him the name was Moran
And that it felt piss-poor. He stared at me like
He'd never seen me before, which of course he hadn't.

Just Joking

Frivolity is the species' refusal to suffer.
—John Lahr

This morning I am fifty-one
(maybe a third of a tank left)
and all the read and spoken words of thirty years
spill like the urgently indifferent tides at Rio del Mar,
only the gags seem somehow to hang on.

Talking Kant with Thalberg was a rich mix,
fueling a friendship with heady afternoons,
but always it was best when we strayed
into the preposterous, sometimes
laughing until the dogs, down in the garden digging,
looked quizzically back at us with adobe-caked noses.

At Father Dunne's the argument was Grace,
which took us late into the merlot hours.
I could not buy his gentle certainties,
but ending those nights swapping limericks
among the jittering sycamores
sealed us friends to the grave.

I think what it comes to is
the bewildered heart in us,
which year by year measuring our slim attainments
with mounting despair still feeds
in its recesses some faint hope, despite

the certain knowledge that what it hopes for
cannot change the tide,

and in these moments, a joke,
shaggy, cosmic, learned or foul,
needs no defense.

Hand-Me-Down Lace

Zihuatanejo

Light of step, broad buttocks rippling,
She glides through the Mercado: Mamacita
Muscle on the move. Her niños scold,
Pant to keep up, flaring in royal train
Behind: perhaps, today, centavos for ices?

A slip of a girl, she debuts at morning Mass,
Princess-proud in hand-me-down lace.
Host mirrored on patent leather shoes.

So soon
She yields to the nervous fire of a boy's touch,
Gives herself to the burning, to the discreet
Nuptials—breathless to be confirming
The eternal motherhood dream.

Too soon she dons
The wrinkles of the wrongness of the world;
Her man-boy, restless, prospect without prospects,
Hangs with the older men in the street below.

Some claim her strength lies in her niños;
Elders say it's a birthright from the Lady:
Divine humility working itself out
In the endless reality of having little—

A blood-gift mother passes on to daughter,
Waiting for her the moment she is born.

April Kitten

Mistress of the oblique
In the hunt, in the hall—
Peripheral mystique,
Privilege in a ball.

Curled in an arm of sun,
Black as a demon's gaze,
Your reign has just begun:
Pure mood of garden days.

Paris, After

Helen, why have you come? To hear your name
Possess the harbor like a hymn again?
Your ships are ages gone, nothing's the same:
The sea stands empty of our gods and men.
You wear the azure gown I favored most;
See there, my blood yet clings at breast and thigh—
O, that our wild blood were alone the cost
Of all we set in motion, you and I!
Ten years your lover, I will tell you this:
You loved your legend only. And when soot
Was all that loomed at Troy, and the shore's hiss
The one sane sound, fields smoking to the root,
You caught the morning tide, sailing apart,
To rest your case on a blind poet's heart.

Dawn with You

Stillness whitening
In the window, ending

Niggling dreams. Your fleece:
Black lightning;

Soft yelps; the tang
Of you peaking

Like oxygen
On live coal flaming,

Long ago taming
Ghosts of the others.

Silent Night

We try, this Christmas Eve, to make things right.
But as we meet and share gifts, once love's token,
Our hug's too keen, our smiles too quick and bright,
And though we speak, the final word's been spoken.

A Balmy Night in Barstow

Ramirez couldn't find a Mexican girl
to his liking in all of Hispanic-brown
Monterey County. As he'd done so often
that summer, he pulled out the frazzled snapshot
of raven-maned Inez, main squeeze of his youth,
and said he needed to head down to Durango
to be with her a while. It was horseshit.
All that was years ago, I reminded him,
and someone that beautiful would be married
by now in a casa crawling with niños—
that or gotten herself to a nunnery
if she'd resolved, when Ramirez split, that if
it couldn't be him it wasn't going to be
anyone short of the Bridegroom of Heaven
Himself. Of course the poet in Ramirez
went for the nun scenario, picturing
veil-of-white-and-candlelight-type stuff.
It was clear he was missing the connection
between a nun's commitment to her God
and her lack of enthusiasm for
a tongue-down-the-throat, hand up the skirt
reunion with her high school indiscretions.

We'd just finished construction on the hotel
going up south of Monterey, and were looking at
a do-nothing week or two before being called
in for a new concrete project. Which meant

Ramirez could finally pull off the love trip.
Since Fugi and I had never so much
as farted in Mexico, we decided
to tag along to see what delights were being
served up south of the border. The likeliest
wheels being my rust-dappled Ford Cheyenne pickup,
we piled into the cab three-across and, on
a sweltering August evening, headed southeast
into the Mojave Desert.

                    Near midnight,
while Ramirez and I dozed, Fugi blew through
the old customs station at Daggett doing
ninety plus on the wrong side of the road.
Wild shouts and cussing told me the driving
lessons I'd given our oriental friend
needed work. Jesus, Fugi, stop! Christ's sake, stop!
It took a quarter mile to get the pickup
out from under his foot and under control.

At this juncture we had company. Bigtime.
An immense customs agent in green bellowed
at the window for Fugi to step out—now.
Fugi, whose English, heard or spoken,
is puke awful, sat stone-faced, petrified.
Mistaking this for go-to-hell defiance,
the giant peeled open the door and commenced
yanking the smart-ass out bodily. Ramirez,
awake finally, uncorked as straight a right jab
as the tight quarters would permit. The big guy,

blood spewing from two flattened nostrils, went down
like a free-falling safe.

                 Unarmed, the other
customs types retreated a step or two
as Ramirez took over the wheel and laid
enough rubber to keep Firestone making tires
for a week. It ended, so much for suspense,
seven miles up 66 when four squad cars
converged on the Shell station where we'd pulled in
for a fast fill. Before they lifted our keys,
wallets, watches, belts, pride, and other personal
effects at the jail, Ramirez got one last
shot in at the Jolly Green Giant who'd hung around
to gloat. Down he went again, hard. Even
the cops had to stifle a laugh.

                 Next morning,
after a what-the-hell-kind-of bug-is-that?
night in the Barstow jail, they threw us our stuff,
said we were taking a ride in the country.
We sweat all the way to a rundown ranch house
outside Daggett where a wintry, one-eyed
judge periodically spat across the room
from his rolltop desk onto a slime-black hearth.
You boys cooled off, have you? he asked, his empty
socket wreathed in a smile. We grinned our docile
best. Good, he said. That'll be six hundred dollars
or sixty days. (Will wonders never cease?
Six hundred and six was what they took when

they booked us.) Before we were out and down
the porch steps, the judge and two of Barstow's
finest were guffawing and splitting the cash.

In the parking lot behind the new cathouse
in Watsonville, Fugi and I waited while
Ramirez got his ashes hauled (he'd hid
a fifty in his shorts). I was drifting off:
Inez, my dear, today you dodged the bola.

Third Daughter

No broom in Cinderella's hands
Or dust cap on her hair. Just you
In your strained peace, tight dental bands,
The millstone, twice, of hand-me-downs;
Flicker of maybe-smile.

Someday, Babe, there'll be the ball.
Likely by accident you'll find it,
Past battered traffic signs and mall;
You probably won't have dressed for it,
Or done any planning at all.

It will be, like suddenly,
A quite unarguable sight.
And like a new moon rising, silver
Of cheek, enthralled at its own light,
You'll steal away from me.

Outside pearled palace rooms and hallways
Where waltzes echo and the mice
And pumpkins run, may spirit power
Your dancing seasons and, as always,
Defy the witching hour.

Early Augustine's Late Taxi

The drear of 5 am
Seeps into Hippo streets.
Arriving on the lam,

Lust, like a riotous bell,
Topping the towers of id,
Exacts its wily toll.

Ah, whoso list to chase,
He knows where is a lair—
Boss pelt, long legs and lace—

And an atoning prayer.

Above Santa Cruz

At my mother's grave

I was nine when the household wept
to see you harden in your bed;
they took me from the darkened room—
by noon came word that you were dead.
Then war called father, and I kept
childhood for another time.

Though new homes gather in these hills,
our bees and a few shadows stay
near this stone above the sea.
Here, on your Irish beauty, clay
settled and, as meaning stilled,
performed the last indignity.

The little time we had should stand
graven, yet this, too, denied,
well-worn memories at the grave,
indistinct and simplified,
became your evening voice and hand:
all that remain of what you gave.

6:30 Mass

(Chicago, early '50s)

Almost too old for sin they wash and come,
Old guests of the late night whose fears endure
Till narrow lamps define their neighboring Rome,
And they find death still splendid and secure,
Nailed in the very flesh it started from.
Springing from stone with arms that could be real,
Forever urgent, yet forever dumb,
Saint Michael and the angels stoop to heal.
Soon gray lips hard with Latin in the chill
Accept the thin cold body in whose patience
They consummate the terrors of the Hill—
While doubt, defunct in all but motion, moves
From where for twenty centuries in silence
Mary's pale face is turned among her doves.

Here's Looking at Us

For Hugo Theimer

. . . as we admire the cunning of Frank Lloyd Wright,
his houses so at ease in the land around them
they almost pass for earth's own ideas—
as if their one-now-with-nature owners
might do life secure as mineral;

regard the mending CEO, teaching now,
ending minimum days with a stroll home
through campus neighborhoods, his furrowed wife,
part of it this time, waiting in porch shadows
with lemonade and harmless local news;

witness "With Someone Like You" souls headed West,
dumping urban playgrounds for the fabled
fellowship of a Rocky Mountain smile,
deer pausing on knolls, radios airing
real country music—three chords and the truth;

and the very old, shrunken in seaside condos—
doorman stationed below to turn away
inflation—roaming salt-rusted terraces,
ghosts of childhood calling back from darkness
sandcastle dawns, the innocent morning wave.

The Play's the Sting

Love's Labour's Lost: you played a blackamoor,
remember? Darling of Ashland and the critics
that year, a drop-dead female cynosure—
the cryptic smile, the bold mischievous antics,

breaths held as footlights stroked your gleaming torso.
Though you were slave, no lady was your peer.
I loved you desperately. By morning more so.
Then you were gone without a note. The year

brought no chance meetings, no belated claim
to jar existing ties. I, not in spite,
left off at last, willing my hermit flame
to late leaves turning in the autumn light.

My tameless temptresses and blackamoors
were lost again among the household chores.

Imaginary Voyages III

Madame de Pompadour puts in at Martinique

Your heat, Madame, is patient, eternal.
Your summons unending.
The sea groans its love through coral loins,
Champagne tides simmer on high beaches.
Your shoulders sleeken to near-Carib gold,
Suffering Everyman's hunger—
O, impudent afternoons!

But royal purples fade in sour winds;
The tribal dance grows vengeful, wild,
You eye your primal grace in tidal pools
And smile: yours are the moves
To tame a Carib king—moves that yet keep
The Versailles Bourbon all but stupefied.

Dog Days in Puerto Vallarta

In shaggy, ranging fellowship
They come at seven in the morning
Already panting steam
At the steaming clay stones:
Thin pickings.

Church, market, bakery richly
Exhale in humid hollows.

By nine, every old trail clean,
New promises pried,
They gather beside the sweating sea
With taxi-mashed or outright
Missing paws.

A fisherwoman who stops
To laugh at them,
Old banditos, sea-soaked, sand-costumed,
Earnestly fishing out their days,
Soon scurries on like the austere crab.

Long after sundown
You can see them still tumbling
In the tide, butter fangs
Closing on the empty wave.

Not Regardless of My Love

Not regardless of my love,
Or the spirit in the dove
Who, for Saint John by the sea,
Simplified eternity,

I have listened as your claims,
First forsworn by Roman names,
Sidestepped now by dull respect
Wait in silence and neglect.

God forgive my intellect.

Boot Camp

To Kevin Andrew Murphy

Wild tales of frontline carnage spread,
and talismans we each would keep
finger-close even in our sleep.
So for a spell we'd ditch the dead.

Reason was not at hand. We served
in those mad months the worst of sense,
till what we feared most we innerved:
a new and awful competence.

So for a spell we ditched the dead—
finger-close even in our sleep,
and talismans we each would keep.
Wild tales of frontline carnage spread.

Parish Girls

They cruise the carnival in bands
where giant Andy Pandas rule—
stuffed rewards for the deft ring toss . . .
dime blitzing . . . silver hopes . . .
ringer! And a smother-hugging

of Andy (who keeps his cool).
Queenly they feel on the Ferris wheel,
unzipped on the Zipper . . . blouses awry,
stockings loopy . . . frantic repairs
as the boys arrive with slicing eyes

fresh from Friday confession.
Octopus, under a moon grown full,
curls them up church walls and steeple.
Screaming, paling, beaming, they pull
the cotton candy beard of God.

Horseman, 5:14

I am exhumed on the express,
Out of the aftermath of five,
And though I starve on consciousness,
Dead reckoning keeps me alive.

Transient, I ride like sun on chrome.
Velocity, my brightest skill,
Sustains me like an ordered home;
Meaning is individual.

As the enigma deepens, I,
Who hunt on plains of sensory error,
Mete out the judgment of my eye
And multiply in finite terror.

My love is waiting near her bed,
Great shadows fall upon the West;
Train, freighted with tomorrow's dead,
Take me to fury, not to rest.

Sleeping Beauty

After Valéry

She sleeps in a palace of rose innocence
Under day's murmurs in the slow vine's hold;
From coral walls is culled an utterance
When stray birds come and pick at her rings of gold.
She does not hear the silver rains that fall
Through palace silences, nor could she bear,
In the east wood, the flute's insistent call
Rife with sweet rumors of awakening there.

Prodigal sunsets dote upon her, till,
Racing to reassert its old hauteur,
A late persimmon moon scatters its chill.
No, nothing here is known—nothing to learn,
Only time's cadence which will never stir
In her French arms the tendons of concern.

The Way of the Cross

At El Retiro San Inigo

Sweet Trumpeter, jammed at last by pitchy Bugles,
Hunting the chance face that yet might hear,
Minstrel, whose strange and tender song hangs
In the land, what notes have frozen in your throat?
    Look, he is down! The Jew king has fallen!

I see you, wild-eyed, face to face with your
Mother, who neither can stop you nor
Let you pass, her breasts remembering
Your infant lips, her lips remembering . . .
    He is down! The Jew king is down!

Once carpenter, you marvel when the spike
Meets no resistance in your wrist. Hushed
At last—a freeze-frame for all time—the crowd
Lifts its impatient face to a nuisance dying.
    After today, history has few surprises.

Holy Thursday

Tonight I ask You in to help me mourn.
You who help whom You please,
don't leave me just with these—
a loincloth, timber, nail, and scarlet thorn.

I'm what I earn to think, not think I am.
Nor love, wisdom, or art
sustains the baffled heart,
and fact contains no holy anagram.

Be more, Lord, than my hope, Your innocence.
Reason has never known
how to live with its own
immaculate, hard-hearted arguments.

Nightpiece

To my newborn son

Welcome, Michael—our home.
　　Delight has left us all but numb!
Above the park, to this room,
　　love at last has come.

Your tiny fist strikes out at noise
　　womb's dark would not admit—
first rites of self, genetic poise
　　securing what the darkness knit.

Pines hush and brighten at the moon,
　　fat stars high-step across the night;
to you, small one, be ever drawn
　　the promises of light.

This hour we are beyond all harm
　　except I dare to hold
Cognizance—weightless, watchful, warm:
　　the tyranny of three days old.

The Other Cheek

The other cheek, as old age nears,
turns grudgingly. Illusions end.
With luck old attitudes unbend
to a poise patient of the years.

In time we outfox grief. And pain
—O, merciless and sly comrade!—
though you would muscle mankind mad,
the hurt have ways of staying sane.

Some, keen about redemption, speak
of Satan and his wily work;
others prepare a coffin smirk
and offer up a different cheek.

Old Silver

To Pat again

Buffing the cherry wood, old silver,
Pitted hopes, stitching sweet hints of you into
Pillow, duvet as agate skies howl,
Always you have looked at me with love,

And practiced for my sake your beauty—
Shy, yearbook smile revisiting
Chestnut eyes when we return to the flesh
For a time, ignoring the soul wrinkles.

How gracefully you greet time's
Non-ovations, which come like vagrants to feed
In our commitment of days,
Your style ever steady against the years.

Today in Time

Today I turned in time, the door
Closed on my late friend sixty-four;
He will not call again before
I lock up and receive no more.
Someone tell me—what are friends for?

CPSIA information can be obtained
at www.ICGtesting.com
Printed in the USA
FFOW03n0135240917
40197FF